EMMANUEL JOSEPH

The Psychology of Progress, How Politics, Health, and Business Shape Social Change

Copyright © 2025 by Emmanuel Joseph

All rights reserved. No part of this publication may be reproduced, stored or transmitted in any form or by any means, electronic, mechanical, photocopying, recording, scanning, or otherwise without written permission from the publisher. It is illegal to copy this book, post it to a website, or distribute it by any other means without permission.

First edition

This book was professionally typeset on Reedsy.
Find out more at reedsy.com

Contents

1. Chapter 1: The Foundations of Progress — 1
2. Chapter 2: Political Ideologies and Social Change — 3
3. Chapter 3: The Role of Political Leadership — 5
4. Chapter 4: Health and Societal Well-Being — 7
5. Chapter 5: The Psychology of Economic Development — 9
6. Chapter 6: The Role of Technology in Social Change — 11
7. Chapter 7: The Intersection of Politics and Health — 13
8. Chapter 8: The Business of Health — 15
9. Chapter 9: The Impact of Globalization on Social Change — 17
10. Chapter 10: The Psychology of Environmental Sustainability — 19
11. Chapter 11: The Role of Education in Social Change — 21
12. Chapter 12: The Role of Media in Social Change — 23
13. Chapter 13: The Psychology of Innovation — 25
14. Chapter 14: The Impact of Social Movements on Progress — 27
15. Chapter 15: The Psychology of Resistance to Change — 29
16. Chapter 16: The Role of Policy in Social Change — 31
17. Chapter 17: The Future of Social Change — 33

1

Chapter 1: The Foundations of Progress

Progress is a multifaceted concept that has driven humanity forward for centuries. It is the pursuit of better living conditions, the quest for knowledge, and the desire to create a more just and equitable society. Understanding the foundations of progress requires an examination of the interplay between politics, health, and business. These three pillars have been instrumental in shaping social change, influencing the way societies evolve and adapt to new challenges. By delving into the historical, psychological, and social dimensions of progress, we can gain a deeper appreciation for the forces that drive human development.

The role of politics in progress cannot be overstated. Political institutions and leaders have the power to enact policies that promote social change, address inequalities, and foster economic growth. Throughout history, political movements have challenged the status quo, advocating for reforms that have transformed societies. From the abolition of slavery to the fight for civil rights, political activism has been a catalyst for progress, pushing boundaries and redefining societal norms. Understanding the psychology behind political movements and leadership is essential for comprehending how political forces shape social change.

Health is another critical factor in the psychology of progress. Advances in medical science and public health have played a pivotal role in improving the quality of life for millions of people worldwide. The eradication of deadly diseases, the development of vaccines, and the promotion of healthier lifestyles have all contributed to significant social change. The psychological impact of health on progress is profound, as healthier populations are better equipped to contribute to economic growth, political stability, and social cohesion. By examining the relationship between health and progress, we can better understand the importance of investing in healthcare and public health initiatives.

Business and economics are the third pillar of progress. The rise of capitalism, industrialization, and globalization have all had a profound impact on social change. Economic growth and development have led to increased living standards, technological advancements, and greater access to education and opportunities. The psychology of business and entrepreneurship is essential for understanding how economic forces drive progress. The motivations, behaviors, and decisions of business leaders and entrepreneurs have far-reaching implications for society, shaping the way we live, work, and interact with one another.

2

Chapter 2: Political Ideologies and Social Change

Political ideologies are the bedrock of social change. They provide the framework through which individuals and groups interpret the world, guiding their actions and shaping their goals. From liberalism to conservatism, socialism to capitalism, political ideologies have a profound impact on the direction of societal progress. By exploring the psychological underpinnings of these ideologies, we can better understand how they influence social change and the ways in which they manifest in political movements and policies.

Liberalism, with its emphasis on individual freedoms and equality, has been a driving force behind many progressive movements. The quest for civil rights, gender equality, and LGBTQ+ rights are all rooted in liberal ideals. The psychological appeal of liberalism lies in its promise of personal autonomy and social justice, resonating with individuals who seek to challenge oppressive systems and create a more inclusive society. Understanding the motivations behind liberal activism can provide valuable insights into the dynamics of social change.

Conservatism, on the other hand, emphasizes tradition, stability, and the preservation of established institutions. The psychological appeal of conservatism lies in its promise of order and continuity, resonating with individuals who value social cohesion and cultural heritage. Conservative movements often arise in response to perceived threats to the status quo, advocating for policies that maintain existing power structures and resist radical change. By examining the psychological foundations of conservatism, we can gain a deeper understanding of the resistance to progressive reforms and the ways in which conservative ideologies shape social change.

Socialism and capitalism represent two opposing economic ideologies that have had a profound impact on social change. Socialism advocates for collective ownership and the equitable distribution of resources, seeking to address economic inequalities and promote social welfare. The psychological appeal of socialism lies in its promise of social justice and economic security, resonating with individuals who seek to challenge the concentration of wealth and power. Capitalism, on the other hand, emphasizes free markets, competition, and individual entrepreneurship. The psychological appeal of capitalism lies in its promise of economic freedom and upward mobility, resonating with individuals who value personal initiative and innovation. By exploring the psychological foundations of these economic ideologies, we can better understand their influence on social change.

3

Chapter 3: The Role of Political Leadership

Political leadership plays a crucial role in shaping social change. The decisions and actions of political leaders have far-reaching implications for society, influencing policies, public opinion, and the direction of progress. Understanding the psychology of political leadership is essential for comprehending how leaders inspire, motivate, and mobilize people to achieve social change.

Charismatic leadership is one of the most powerful drivers of social change. Charismatic leaders possess a unique ability to connect with people on an emotional level, inspiring loyalty and devotion. Their vision and passion can galvanize movements, mobilize supporters, and challenge entrenched power structures. The psychological appeal of charismatic leadership lies in its promise of transformative change and the creation of a better future. By examining the characteristics and behaviors of charismatic leaders, we can gain insights into how they shape social change.

Transformational leadership is another key aspect of political leadership. Transformational leaders seek to create positive change by empowering and inspiring others. They focus on developing a shared vision, fostering collaboration, and encouraging innovation. The psychological appeal of transformational leadership lies in its emphasis on personal growth and collective empowerment, resonating with individuals who seek to contribute to the greater good. Understanding the dynamics of transformational leadership can provide valuable insights into how political leaders drive social change.

Leadership in times of crisis is a critical aspect of political leadership. Crises, whether they be economic, social, or environmental, require decisive and effective leadership to navigate. The psychological impact of crisis leadership is profound, as leaders must manage fear, uncertainty, and anxiety while guiding society through challenging times. By examining the strategies and behaviors of successful crisis leaders, we can better understand how they shape social change and contribute to progress.

4

Chapter 4: Health and Societal Well-Being

Health is a fundamental component of societal well-being and progress. The relationship between health and social change is complex and multifaceted, with advances in medical science and public health having a profound impact on the quality of life and societal development. By examining the psychological dimensions of health, we can gain a deeper understanding of how health influences social change and the ways in which health initiatives contribute to progress.

The psychology of health behavior is essential for understanding how individuals and communities adopt healthier lifestyles. Health behaviors, such as diet, exercise, and smoking cessation, are influenced by a range of psychological factors, including motivation, self-efficacy, and social norms. By exploring the psychological foundations of health behavior, we can develop more effective interventions and policies to promote healthier lifestyles and improve public health.

Mental health is another critical aspect of societal well-being. The psychological impact of mental health on progress is significant, as mental health disorders can affect individuals' ability to contribute to society, maintain relationships, and achieve personal goals. By examining the relationship between mental health and social change, we can better understand the importance of mental health initiatives and the role of mental health professionals in promoting societal well-being.

Public health initiatives play a vital role in shaping social change. The promotion of vaccination, disease prevention, and health education have all contributed to significant improvements in public health and quality of life. The psychological impact of public health initiatives is profound, as healthier populations are better equipped to contribute to economic growth, political stability, and social cohesion. By exploring the relationship between public health and progress, we can gain valuable insights into the importance of investing in healthcare and public health initiatives.

5

Chapter 5: The Psychology of Economic Development

Economic development is a key driver of social change, influencing living standards, access to education, and opportunities for personal and professional growth. The psychology of economic development is essential for understanding how economic forces shape progress and the ways in which individuals and communities respond to economic challenges and opportunities.

The motivation behind entrepreneurship and innovation is a critical aspect of economic development. Entrepreneurs and innovators play a vital role in driving economic growth, creating jobs, and fostering technological advancements. The psychological appeal of entrepreneurship lies in its promise of economic freedom and upward mobility, resonating with individuals who value personal initiative and creativity. By examining the psychological foundations of entrepreneurship, we can better understand the motivations and behaviors of business leaders and their impact on social change.

The role of education and skill development in economic development is another critical aspect of progress. Access to quality education and opportunities for skill development are essential for creating a more equitable and prosperous society. The psychological impact of education on progress is profound, as educated individuals are better equipped to contribute to economic growth, political stability, and social cohesion. By exploring the relationship between education and economic development, we can gain valuable insights into the importance of investing in education and training initiatives.

The psychology of consumer behavior is also essential for understanding economic development. Consumer behavior is influenced by a range of psychological factors, including motivation, perception, and social norms. By examining the psychological foundations of consumer behavior, we can better understand how individuals and communities make economic decisions and the ways in which these decisions shape progress.

6

Chapter 6: The Role of Technology in Social Change

Technology has been a driving force behind social change for centuries, revolutionizing the way we live, work, and interact with one another. The psychology of technology is essential for understanding how technological advancements influence progress and the ways in which individuals and communities adapt to new technologies.

The psychological impact of technological innovation is profound, as new technologies can create both opportunities and challenges for society. Technological advancements have the potential to improve living standards, increase access to information, and foster economic growth. However, they can also lead to social and economic inequalities, disrupt traditional industries, and create ethical dilemmas. By examining the psychological foundations of technological innovation, we can better understand the impact of technology on social change and the ways in which individuals and communities adapt to new technologies.

The role of artificial intelligence (AI) in social change is a significant aspect of technological innovation. AI has the potential to transform industries, improve decision-making processes, and enhance the quality of life. However, it also raises ethical concerns and challenges related to privacy, employment, and security. The psychological impact of AI on progress is profound, as it influences the way individuals and communities perceive and interact with technology. By examining the psychological foundations of AI, we can better understand its impact on social change and the ways in which society can harness its potential for progress.

The digital divide is another critical aspect of technology and social change. The unequal access to technology and digital resources can exacerbate existing social and economic inequalities, creating barriers to progress for marginalized communities. The psychological impact of the digital divide is significant, as it affects individuals' ability to participate in the digital economy, access information, and engage with social and political processes. By exploring the psychological dimensions of the digital divide, we can develop more effective strategies to promote digital inclusion and bridge the gap between different social groups.

7

Chapter 7: The Intersection of Politics and Health

The intersection of politics and health is a crucial aspect of social change. Political decisions and policies have a profound impact on public health, influencing access to healthcare, the distribution of resources, and the promotion of healthy behaviors. Understanding the psychology of political decision-making in the context of health is essential for comprehending how political forces shape social change and the ways in which health initiatives contribute to progress.

The role of government in healthcare is a critical aspect of the intersection between politics and health. Governments have the power to enact policies that promote public health, provide access to healthcare services, and address health inequalities. The psychological impact of government involvement in healthcare is significant, as it influences individuals' perceptions of the healthcare system and their trust in political institutions. By examining the relationship between government policies and public health, we can gain valuable insights into the ways in which political decisions shape social change and contribute to societal well-being.

The impact of political activism on health is another critical aspect of the intersection between politics and health. Political activism has been instrumental in advocating for health reforms, challenging oppressive systems, and promoting public health initiatives. The psychological appeal of health activism lies in its promise of social justice and the creation of a healthier society, resonating with individuals who seek to address health inequalities and improve public health. By exploring the motivations and behaviors of health activists, we can better understand the dynamics of social change and the ways in which political movements contribute to progress.

The role of international organizations in health is another critical aspect of the intersection between politics and health. International organizations, such as the World Health Organization (WHO) and the United Nations (UN), play a vital role in promoting global health initiatives, coordinating responses to health crises, and addressing health inequalities. The psychological impact of international organizations on progress is significant, as they influence the way individuals and communities perceive global health issues and their trust in international institutions. By examining the relationship between international organizations and health, we can gain valuable insights into the ways in which global health initiatives contribute to social change and progress.

8

Chapter 8: The Business of Health

The business of health is a critical aspect of social change, influencing access to healthcare, the development of medical technologies, and the promotion of healthier lifestyles. The psychology of the healthcare industry is essential for understanding how economic forces shape progress and the ways in which individuals and communities respond to health challenges and opportunities.

The role of pharmaceutical companies in health is a significant aspect of the business of health. Pharmaceutical companies play a vital role in developing and distributing medications, vaccines, and medical technologies that improve public health and quality of life. The psychological impact of pharmaceutical companies on progress is profound, as their innovations have the potential to address health challenges, reduce disease burden, and enhance societal well-being. However, the pharmaceutical industry also faces ethical challenges related to pricing, access, and transparency. By examining the psychological foundations of the pharmaceutical industry, we can better understand its impact on social change and the ways in which it contributes to progress.

The impact of the healthcare industry on economic development is another critical aspect of the business of health. The healthcare industry is a significant driver of economic growth, creating jobs, fostering innovation, and contributing to economic stability. The psychological appeal of the healthcare industry lies in its promise of economic security and improved quality of life, resonating with individuals who value personal health and well-being. By exploring the relationship between the healthcare industry and economic development, we can gain valuable insights into the ways in which economic forces shape progress and contribute to social change.

The role of health insurance in promoting access to healthcare is another critical aspect of the business of health. Health insurance plays a vital role in reducing financial barriers to healthcare, providing access to essential services, and promoting health equity. The psychological impact of health insurance on progress is significant, as it influences individuals' perceptions of the healthcare system and their trust in economic institutions. By examining the relationship between health insurance and access to healthcare, we can better understand the ways in which economic policies shape social change and contribute to societal well-being.

9

Chapter 9: The Impact of Globalization on Social Change

Globalization has been a driving force behind social change for centuries, influencing the way societies interact, trade, and develop. The psychology of globalization is essential for understanding how global forces shape progress and the ways in which individuals and communities adapt to new challenges and opportunities.

The role of international trade in globalization is a significant aspect of social change. International trade has the potential to promote economic growth, create jobs, and improve living standards. However, it can also lead to social and economic inequalities, disrupt traditional industries, and create ethical dilemmas. The psychological impact of international trade on progress is profound, as it influences the way individuals and communities perceive and interact with global markets. By examining the psychological foundations of international trade, we can better understand its impact on social change and the ways in which society can harness its potential for progress.

The impact of migration on social change is another critical aspect of globalization. Migration has the potential to enrich societies, promote cultural exchange, and contribute to economic development. However, it can also create social tensions, exacerbate inequalities, and challenge social cohesion. The psychological impact of migration on progress is significant, as it influences individuals' perceptions of diversity, identity, and belonging. By exploring the psychological dimensions of migration, we can better understand the ways in which migration shapes social change and the ways in which societies can promote inclusion and integration.

The role of international organizations in globalization is another critical aspect of social change. International organizations play a vital role in promoting global cooperation, addressing global challenges, and fostering social change. The psychological impact of international organizations on progress is significant, as they influence the way individuals and communities perceive global issues and their trust in international institutions. By examining the relationship between international organizations and globalization, we can gain valuable insights into the ways in which global cooperation contributes to social change and progress.

10

Chapter 10: The Psychology of Environmental Sustainability

Environmental sustainability is a critical aspect of social change, influencing the way societies interact with the natural world and address environmental challenges. The psychology of environmental sustainability is essential for understanding how individuals and communities perceive and respond to environmental issues and the ways in which environmental initiatives contribute to progress.

The impact of environmental awareness on social change is significant, as it influences individuals' attitudes and behaviors toward the environment. Environmental awareness campaigns and education initiatives have the potential to promote sustainable practices, reduce environmental impact, and foster a culture of environmental stewardship. The psychological appeal of environmental awareness lies in its promise of a healthier and more sustainable future, resonating with individuals who value personal and collective responsibility for the environment. By examining the psychological foundations of environmental awareness, we can better understand its impact on social change and the ways in which society can promote environmental sustainability.

The role of environmental policies in promoting sustainability is another critical aspect of environmental sustainability. Governments and international organizations have the power to enact policies that promote sustainable practices, address environmental challenges, and reduce environmental impact. The psychological impact of environmental policies on progress is significant, as they influence individuals' perceptions of the environment and their trust in political institutions. By examining the relationship between environmental policies and sustainability, we can gain valuable insights into the ways in which political decisions shape social change and contribute to environmental progress.

The impact of green technologies on environmental sustainability is another critical aspect of social change. Green technologies, such as renewable energy, energy-efficient buildings, and sustainable transportation, have the potential to reduce environmental impact and promote sustainable development. The psychological appeal of green technologies lies in their promise of innovation and progress, resonating with individuals who value technological advancements and environmental responsibility. By exploring the relationship between green technologies and sustainability, we can better understand their impact on social change and the ways in which society can harness their potential for progress.

11

Chapter 11: The Role of Education in Social Change

Education is a fundamental component of social change, influencing individuals' attitudes, behaviors, and opportunities for personal and professional growth. The psychology of education is essential for understanding how educational initiatives shape progress and the ways in which individuals and communities respond to educational challenges and opportunities.

The impact of access to education on social change is significant, as it influences individuals' ability to participate in the economy, engage with social and political processes, and achieve personal goals. Access to quality education is essential for creating a more equitable and prosperous society, promoting social mobility, and reducing inequalities. The psychological appeal of education lies in its promise of personal growth and empowerment, resonating with individuals who seek to improve their lives and contribute to society. By examining the relationship between access to education and social change, we can better understand the ways in which educational initiatives contribute to progress and societal well-being.

The role of educational policies in promoting social change is another critical aspect of education. Governments and international organizations have the power to enact policies that promote access to education, improve educational quality, and address educational inequalities. The psychological impact of educational policies on progress is significant, as they influence individuals' perceptions of the education system and their trust in political institutions. By examining the relationship between educational policies and social change, we can gain valuable insights into the ways in which political decisions shape progress and contribute to educational development.

The impact of innovative teaching methods on social change is another critical aspect of education. Innovative teaching methods, such as experiential learning, project-based learning, and technology-enhanced education, have the potential to improve educational outcomes, foster creativity, and promote critical thinking. The psychological appeal of innovative teaching methods lies in their promise of engaging and effective learning experiences, resonating with individuals who value personal growth and lifelong learning. By exploring the relationship between innovative teaching methods and social change, we can better understand the ways in which educational innovations contribute to progress and societal well-being.

12

Chapter 12: The Role of Media in Social Change

The media is a powerful force in shaping social change, influencing public opinion, disseminating information, and holding institutions accountable. The psychology of media is essential for understanding how media content and communication strategies shape progress and the ways in which individuals and communities respond to media messages.

The impact of news media on social change is significant, as it influences individuals' perceptions of current events, political issues, and societal challenges. News media plays a crucial role in informing the public, raising awareness of social issues, and fostering public discourse. The psychological appeal of news media lies in its promise of truth and accountability, resonating with individuals who value transparency and informed decision-making. By examining the relationship between news media and social change, we can gain valuable insights into the ways in which media coverage shapes public opinion and contributes to progress.

The role of social media in promoting social change is another critical aspect of media. Social media platforms have revolutionized the way individuals and communities communicate, mobilize, and advocate for social change. The psychological impact of social media on progress is profound, as it enables individuals to share their experiences, connect with like-minded individuals, and amplify their voices. By exploring the relationship between social media and social change, we can better understand the ways in which digital communication fosters activism, empowers marginalized communities, and contributes to societal progress.

The influence of entertainment media on social change is another critical aspect of media. Movies, television shows, music, and literature have the power to shape cultural norms, challenge stereotypes, and promote social change. The psychological appeal of entertainment media lies in its promise of emotional engagement and cultural representation, resonating with individuals who seek to see their experiences and identities reflected in media content. By examining the relationship between entertainment media and social change, we can gain valuable insights into the ways in which media content influences societal attitudes and behaviors, and contributes to progress.

13

Chapter 13: The Psychology of Innovation

Innovation is a key driver of social change, influencing technological advancements, economic development, and societal progress. The psychology of innovation is essential for understanding how individuals and communities perceive and respond to new ideas, and the ways in which innovation contributes to progress.

The impact of creativity on innovation is significant, as it influences individuals' ability to generate new ideas, solve problems, and drive progress. Creativity is a critical component of innovation, fostering the development of new technologies, products, and services that improve quality of life and promote social change. The psychological appeal of creativity lies in its promise of novelty and discovery, resonating with individuals who value personal and collective growth. By examining the relationship between creativity and innovation, we can better understand the ways in which creative thinking contributes to progress and societal well-being.

The role of collaboration in innovation is another critical aspect of social change. Collaboration fosters the exchange of ideas, knowledge, and resources, enabling individuals and communities to work together to achieve common goals. The psychological appeal of collaboration lies in its promise of collective empowerment and shared success, resonating with individuals who value teamwork and cooperation. By exploring the relationship between collaboration and innovation, we can gain valuable insights into the ways in which collaborative efforts drive progress and contribute to social change.

The influence of organizational culture on innovation is another critical aspect of social change. Organizational culture shapes the attitudes, behaviors, and values of individuals within an organization, influencing their ability to innovate and drive progress. The psychological impact of organizational culture on innovation is significant, as it affects individuals' motivation, creativity, and willingness to take risks. By examining the relationship between organizational culture and innovation, we can better understand the ways in which supportive and inclusive cultures foster innovation and contribute to societal progress.

14

Chapter 14: The Impact of Social Movements on Progress

Social movements have been instrumental in driving social change, challenging oppressive systems, and advocating for justice and equality. The psychology of social movements is essential for understanding how collective action shapes progress and the ways in which individuals and communities respond to social challenges.

The role of grassroots activism in social movements is significant, as it empowers individuals to take action and advocate for change at the local level. Grassroots activism is driven by the passion and commitment of ordinary people who seek to address social injustices and promote progress. The psychological appeal of grassroots activism lies in its promise of personal empowerment and collective impact, resonating with individuals who value community engagement and social justice. By examining the relationship between grassroots activism and social change, we can gain valuable insights into the ways in which local efforts contribute to progress and societal well-being.

The impact of mass mobilization on social movements is another critical aspect of progress. Mass mobilization involves the large-scale participation of individuals in social movements, amplifying their voices and increasing their influence on public opinion and political decision-making. The psychological appeal of mass mobilization lies in its promise of collective power and societal transformation, resonating with individuals who seek to create a more just and equitable society. By exploring the relationship between mass mobilization and social change, we can better understand the ways in which collective action drives progress and contributes to societal development.

The role of social media in social movements is another critical aspect of progress. Social media platforms have revolutionized the way social movements organize, communicate, and mobilize supporters. The psychological impact of social media on social movements is profound, as it enables individuals to share their experiences, connect with like-minded individuals, and amplify their voices. By examining the relationship between social media and social movements, we can gain valuable insights into the ways in which digital communication fosters activism and contributes to social change.

15

Chapter 15: The Psychology of Resistance to Change

Resistance to change is a natural and common response to social change, as individuals and communities seek to maintain stability and preserve their existing values and norms. The psychology of resistance to change is essential for understanding how individuals and communities perceive and respond to social challenges and the ways in which resistance shapes progress.

The impact of cognitive dissonance on resistance to change is significant, as it influences individuals' ability to reconcile conflicting beliefs and attitudes. Cognitive dissonance occurs when individuals experience discomfort due to conflicting beliefs, leading them to resist new information or changes that challenge their existing views. The psychological impact of cognitive dissonance on resistance to change is profound, as it affects individuals' willingness to adopt new ideas and behaviors. By examining the relationship between cognitive dissonance and resistance to change, we can gain valuable insights into the ways in which individuals and communities respond to social challenges and the ways in which resistance shapes progress.

The role of social identity in resistance to change is another critical aspect of social change. Social identity refers to individuals' sense of belonging to a particular group, influencing their attitudes and behaviors toward social change. The psychological impact of social identity on resistance to change is significant, as it affects individuals' willingness to accept new ideas and behaviors that challenge their group's values and norms. By exploring the relationship between social identity and resistance to change, we can better understand the ways in which group dynamics influence social change and the ways in which resistance shapes progress.

The influence of fear and uncertainty on resistance to change is another critical aspect of social change. Fear and uncertainty can lead individuals to resist new ideas and behaviors, as they seek to maintain stability and avoid potential risks. The psychological impact of fear and uncertainty on resistance to change is profound, as it affects individuals' ability to adapt to new challenges and opportunities. By examining the relationship between fear, uncertainty, and resistance to change, we can gain valuable insights into the ways in which individuals and communities respond to social challenges and the ways in which resistance shapes progress.

16

Chapter 16: The Role of Policy in Social Change

Policy plays a crucial role in shaping social change, influencing public opinion, and driving progress. The psychology of policy is essential for understanding how political decisions and policies shape progress and the ways in which individuals and communities respond to policy initiatives.

The impact of policy design on social change is significant, as it influences the effectiveness and acceptance of policy initiatives. Effective policy design involves understanding the needs and preferences of individuals and communities, developing evidence-based solutions, and promoting stakeholder engagement. The psychological appeal of well-designed policies lies in their promise of positive change and societal improvement, resonating with individuals who value effective governance and public service. By examining the relationship between policy design and social change, we can gain valuable insights into the ways in which political decisions shape progress and contribute to societal development.

The role of policy implementation in promoting social change is another critical aspect of progress. Policy implementation involves translating policy decisions into action, ensuring that policies achieve their intended goals and address social challenges. The psychological impact of policy implementation on progress is significant, as it affects individuals' perceptions of the effectiveness and legitimacy of political institutions. By exploring the relationship between policy implementation and social change, we can better understand the ways in which political decisions shape progress and contribute to societal well-being.

The influence of policy evaluation on social change is another critical aspect of progress. Policy evaluation involves assessing the impact and effectiveness of policy initiatives, providing valuable feedback for future policy development. The psychological appeal of policy evaluation lies in its promise of accountability and continuous improvement, resonating with individuals who value transparency and evidence-based decision-making. By examining the relationship between policy evaluation and social change, we can gain valuable insights into the ways in which political decisions shape progress and contribute to societal development.

17

Chapter 17: The Future of Social Change

The future of social change is shaped by a complex interplay of political, economic, social, and technological forces. Understanding the psychology of social change is essential for comprehending how these forces will shape progress and the ways in which individuals and communities will respond to future challenges and opportunities.

The impact of emerging technologies on social change is significant, as technological advancements have the potential to transform industries, improve living standards, and address global challenges. The psychological appeal of emerging technologies lies in their promise of innovation and progress, resonating with individuals who value technological advancements and the potential for positive change. By examining the relationship between emerging technologies and social change, we can gain valuable insights into the ways in which technological innovations will shape the future and contribute to societal progress.

The role of global cooperation in promoting social change is another critical aspect of the future. Global challenges, such as climate change, pandemics, and economic inequalities, require coordinated efforts and international collaboration to address effectively. The psychological impact of global cooperation on progress is significant, as it influences individuals' perceptions of global issues and their trust in international institutions. By exploring the relationship between global cooperation and social change, we can better understand the ways in which collective efforts will shape the future and contribute to societal development.

The influence of social movements on future progress is another critical aspect of social change. Social movements have been instrumental in advocating for justice, equality, and environmental sustainability, challenging oppressive systems, and promoting positive change. The psychological appeal of social movements lies in their promise of collective empowerment and societal transformation, resonating with individuals who seek to create a more just and equitable future. By examining the relationship between social movements and social change, we can gain valuable insights into the ways in which activism and collective action will shape the future and contribute to progress.

Finally, the role of policy in shaping the future is essential for understanding the psychology of social change. Effective policies have the potential to address societal challenges, promote economic development, and foster social cohesion. The psychological impact of well-designed policies on progress is significant, as they influence individuals' perceptions of governance and their trust in political institutions. By exploring the relationship between policy and social change, we can better understand the ways in which political decisions will shape the future and contribute to societal development.

In conclusion, the psychology of progress is a multifaceted and dynamic field, encompassing the interplay of politics, health, and business in shaping social change. By examining the historical, psychological, and social dimensions of progress, we can gain a deeper appreciation for the forces that drive human development and the ways in which individuals and communities respond to future challenges and opportunities. The future of social change will be shaped by emerging technologies, global cooperation, social movements, and effective policies, all of which will contribute to the ongoing pursuit of a more just, equitable, and prosperous society.

Description

"The Psychology of Progress: How Politics, Health, and Business Shape Social Change" delves into the intricate forces that drive societal advancement. This enlightening book explores the critical roles politics, health, and business

CHAPTER 17: THE FUTURE OF SOCIAL CHANGE

play in influencing social change and shaping our collective future. With a focus on the psychological dimensions of these domains, the book examines how political ideologies, leadership, health initiatives, economic development, and technological innovations contribute to progress.

The book is divided into 17 chapters, each offering a deep dive into various aspects of progress, including political ideologies, the intersection of politics and health, the business of health, the role of education, and the impact of social movements. Through a comprehensive analysis, the book provides valuable insights into how individuals and communities respond to challenges and opportunities, driving societal transformation.

By understanding the psychology behind progress, readers will gain a deeper appreciation for the forces that shape our world and the ways in which we can harness these forces to create a more just, equitable, and prosperous society. "The Psychology of Progress" is an essential read for anyone interested in the dynamics of social change and the interplay between politics, health, and business in shaping our collective future.

www.ingramcontent.com/pod-product-compliance
Lightning Source LLC
LaVergne TN
LVHW020459080526
838202LV00057B/6048